2018 SQA Past Papers with Answers

Higher
FRENCH

FREE
audio files to accompany this
title can be accessed at
**www.hoddereducation.co.uk/
sqaaudiofiles**
You will find the files listed by
language and level.

2016, 2017 & 2018 Exams

**HODDER
GIBSON**
AN HACHETTE UK COMPANY

This book contains the official 2016, 2017 and 2018 Exams for Higher French, with associated SQA-approved answers modified from the official marking instructions that accompany the paper.

In addition the book contains study skills advice. This advice has been specially commissioned by Hodder Gibson, and has been written by experienced senior teachers and examiners in line with the Higher syllabus and assessment outlines. This is not SQA material but has been devised to provide further guidance for Higher examinations.

Every effort has been made to trace the copyright holders and to obtain their permission for the use of copyright material. Hodder Gibson will be happy to receive information allowing us to rectify any error or omission in future editions.

Hachette UK's policy is to use papers that are natural, renewable and recyclable products and made from wood grown in sustainable forests. The logging and manufacturing processes are expected to conform to the environmental regulations of the country of origin.

Orders: please contact Bookpoint Ltd, 130 Park Drive, Milton Park, Abingdon, Oxon OX14 4SE. Telephone: (44) 01235 827827. Fax: (44) 01235 400454. Lines are open 9.00–5.00, Monday to Saturday, with a 24-hour message answering service. Visit our website at www.hoddereducation.co.uk. Hodder Gibson can also be contacted directly at hoddergibson@hodder.co.uk

This collection first published in 2018 by
Hodder Gibson, an imprint of Hodder Education,
An Hachette UK Company
211 St Vincent Street
Glasgow G2 5QY

Typeset by Aptara, Inc.

Printed in the UK

A catalogue record for this title is available from the British Library

ISBN: 978-1-5104-5610-5

2 1

2019 2018

Introduction

Higher French

The course

The Higher French course aims to enable you to develop the ability to:

- read, listen, talk and write in French
- understand and use French
- apply your knowledge and understanding of the language.

The course offers the opportunity to develop detailed language skills in the real-life contexts of society, learning, employability and culture.

How the course is graded

The course assessment will take the form of a performance and a written exam:

- The performance will be a discussion with your teacher, which will be recorded and marked by your teacher. This is out of 30, but makes up 25% of your final mark.
- The written exam will be sat in May. This book will help you practise for the exam.
- You will find a lot of guidance on tackling the assignment-writing in How to Pass Higher French.

The exams

Reading and Directed Writing

- exam time: 2 hours

Reading

- total marks: 30
- weighting in final grade: 25%
- what you have to do: read a passage of about 600 words, and answer questions about it in English, including an overall purpose question for 20 marks; translate an extract from the passage of about 40 words into English for 10 marks.

Directed Writing

- total marks: 20
- weighting in final grade: 12.5%
- what you have to do: write 150–180 words in French describing a visit you made, or an experience you had, in a French speaking country.

Listening

- exam time: 30 minutes
- total marks: 20
- weighting in final grade: 25%
- what you have to do: listen to a presentation in French, and answer questions about it in English for 8 marks; then listen to a conversation in French, and answer questions about it in English for 12 marks.

How to improve your mark!

Reading

- Read the whole passage, then pick out the key points. Detailed answers are generally required, so pay particular attention to words like assez, très, trop, vraiment and to negatives. Make sure you get the details of numbers, days, times etc. right.
- Use the line numbers above each question to guide you as to where to look for the answer.
- Take care when using dictionaries where a word has more than one meaning. Learn to choose the correct meaning from a list of meanings in a dictionary, and get in the habit of going beyond the headword. Often you will find the whole phrase you are looking for further down the entry.
- Try to answer the specific wording of the question, but do not give a word-for-word translation of the text as a response to the reading comprehension questions, as this often results in an answer which is not in correct English.
- When responding to the questions in the Reading papers, you should be guided by the number of points awarded for each question. You should give as much detail in your answer as you have understood, but should not put down everything which is in the original text, as you are wasting time. The question itself usually indicates the amount of information required by stating in bold, e.g. 'State **two** of them'. If the question says 'Give **any two**', there are more than two possibilities, so choose the two you are happiest with and stick to them.
- The last question before the translation asks you to look at the passage as a whole, then answer a question and provide evidence to back up your answer. It is important to start your answer with your opinion, then select pieces of text from the passage to back up your answer, giving an English version of what is in the passage.
- Look closely at each word in each section of the translation passage, and pay particular attention to the articles and tenses used. Make sure you

include each word in your translation (although translation is not word for word!). Look at marking schemes for translations to give you an idea of what a good translation should look like.

Directed Writing

- Have a quick look at the two choices for writing, and go for the one for which your prepared material will give you most support.

- Consider, carefully, the wording of each bullet point, and make sure any learned material that you use is relevant and appropriate to the bullet point. Make sure you address each part of the first bullet point, and that you are answering the questions asked.

- Use your dictionary only to check the accuracy of what you have written (spelling, genders etc.), not to create and invent new sentences.

- Don't write pieces that are too lengthy, you only need 150–180 words. So stick to about 30 words per bullet point.

- Be aware of the extended criteria to be used in assessing performances in Writing (included on pages 93–94 and pages 95–97 of this book!) so that you know what's required to achieve the good and very good categories in terms of content, accuracy, and range and variety of language.

- Ensure that your handwriting is legible (particularly when writing in French) and distinguish clearly between rough notes and what you wish to be considered as final answers. Make sure you score out your notes!

- You should bear the following points in mind:
  - There are six bullet points to answer: they are not really predictable and vary from year to year, but certain things come up regularly.
  - Each of the six bullet points should have roughly 30 words to address it properly. Don't write too much!
  - You will be assessed on how well you have answered the points, and on the accuracy of your language.
  - If you miss out or fail to address a bullet point correctly, you will lose marks.
  - For a mark of good or very good, you should have some complex language such as longer, varied sentences, adjectives and conjunctions.

Listening

- Your listening skills will improve most with practice. So use the Listening sections in this book several times to get used to the format of the exam.

- Read the questions carefully before the first listening and use them as a means of anticipating the sort of information you will need to extract from the text.

- Not giving enough detail is still a major reason for candidates losing marks. Many answers are correct as far as they go, but don't have enough detail to score marks. The same rules as for Reading apply. Give as much detail as possible in your answers and don't lose marks by writing down numbers, prepositions and question words inaccurately.

- You hear each of the two Listening texts twice only, so make use of the gap between the two recordings to check which specific details you still need for your answers, so your listening is focused.

- Make sure you're able to give accurate answers through confident knowledge of numbers, common adjectives, weather expressions, prepositions and question words, so that some of the 'easier' points of information are not lost through lack of sufficiently accurate details.

- When responding to the questions in the Listening papers, be guided by the number of points awarded for each question, and by the wording of the question. You should give as much detail in your answer as you have understood, but should not write down everything you hear. The question itself usually indicates the amount of information required by stating in bold, e.g. 'Give **two** of them'.

- Be sure to put a line through any notes you have made! Remember you are not allowed a dictionary in the exam! It is probably better to put down any notes in English, as you will not be able to look up words you are not sure of in a dictionary.

Assignment-writing

- You will be asked by your teacher to write an essay of about 250 words on a topic you know. You could be given a choice of topics to write about.

- This will be carried out in class, but sent to SQA to be marked.

- You should have your first draft looked at by your teacher, who will give suggestions on how you might improve it,

- You can then have a second and final attempt at doing the writing.

Good luck!

Remember that the rewards for passing Higher French are well worth it! Your pass will help you get the future you want for yourself. In the exam, be confident in your own ability. If you're not sure how to answer a question, trust your instincts and just give it a go anyway – keep calm and don't panic! GOOD LUCK!

Study Skills – what you need to know to pass exams!

General exam revision: 20 top tips

When preparing for exams, it is easy to feel unsure of where to start or how to revise. This guide to general exam revision provides a good starting place, and, as these are very general tips, they can be applied to all your exams.

1. Start revising in good time.

Don't leave revision until the last minute – this will make you panic and it will be difficult to learn. Make a revision timetable that counts down the weeks to go.

2. Work to a study plan.

Set up sessions of work spread through the weeks ahead. Make sure each session has a focus and a clear purpose. What will you study, when and why? Be realistic about what you can achieve in each session, and don't be afraid to adjust your plans as needed.

3. Make sure you know exactly when your exams are.

Get your exam dates from the SQA website and use the timetable builder tool to create your own exam schedule. You will also get a personalised timetable from your school, but this might not be until close to the exam period.

4. Make sure that you know the topics that make up each course.

Studying is easier if material is in manageable chunks – why not use the SQA topic headings or create your own from your class notes? Ask your teacher for help on this if you are not sure.

5. Break the chunks up into even smaller bits.

The small chunks should be easier to cope with. Remember that they fit together to make larger ideas. Even the process of chunking down will help!

6. Ask yourself these key questions for each course:

- Are all topics compulsory or are there choices?
- Which topics seem to come up time and time again?
- Which topics are your strongest and which are your weakest?

Use your answers to these questions to work out how much time you will need to spend revising each topic.

7. Make sure you know what to expect in the exam.

The subject-specific introduction to this book will help with this. Make sure you can answer these questions:

- How is the paper structured?
- How much time is there for each part of the exam?
- What types of question are involved? These will vary depending on the subject so read the subject-specific section carefully.

8. Past papers are a vital *revision tool!*

Use past papers to support your revision wherever possible. This book contains the answers and mark schemes too – refer to these carefully when checking your work. Using the mark scheme is useful; even if you don't manage to get all the marks available first time when you first practise, it helps you identify how to extend and develop your answers to get more marks next time – and of course, in the real exam.

9. Use study methods that work well for you.

People study and learn in different ways. Reading and looking at diagrams suits some students. Others prefer to listen and hear material – what about reading out loud or getting a friend or family member to do this for you? You could also record and play back material.

10. There are three tried and tested ways to make material stick in your long-term memory:

- Practising – e.g. rehearsal, repeating
- Organising – e.g. making drawings, lists, diagrams, tables, memory aids
- Elaborating – e.g. incorporating the material into a story or an imagined journey

11. Learn actively.

Most people prefer to learn actively – for example, making notes, highlighting, redrawing and redrafting, making up memory aids, or writing past paper answers. A good way to stay engaged and inspired is to mix and match these methods – find the combination that best suits you. This is likely to vary depending on the topic or subject.

12. Be an expert.

Be sure to have a few areas in which you feel you are an expert. This often works because at least some of them will come up, which can boost confidence.

13. Try some visual methods.

Use symbols, diagrams, charts, flashcards, post-it notes etc. Don't forget – the brain takes in chunked images more easily than loads of text.

14. Remember – practice makes perfect.

Work on difficult areas again and again. Look and read – then test yourself. You cannot do this too much.

15. Try past papers against the clock.

Practise writing answers in a set time. This is a good habit from the start but is especially important when you get closer to exam time.

16. Collaborate with friends.

Test each other and talk about the material – this can really help. Two brains are better than one! It is amazing how talking about a problem can help you solve it.

17. Know your weaknesses.

Ask your teacher for help to identify what you don't know. Try to do this as early as possible. If you are having trouble, it is probably with a difficult topic, so your teacher will already be aware of this – most students will find it tough.

18. Have your materials organised and ready.

Know what is needed for each exam:

- Do you need a calculator or a ruler?
- Should you have pencils as well as pens?
- Will you need water or paper tissues?

19. Make full use of school resources.

Find out what support is on offer:

- Are there study classes available?
- When is the library open?
- When is the best time to ask for extra help?
- Can you borrow textbooks, study guides, past papers, etc.?
- Is school open for Easter revision?

20. Keep fit and healthy!

Try to stick to a routine as much as possible, including with sleep. If you are tired, sluggish or dehydrated, it is difficult to see how concentration is even possible. Combine study with relaxation, drink plenty of water, eat sensibly, and get fresh air and exercise – all these things will help more than you could imagine. Good luck!

HIGHER

2016

X730/76/11

**French
Reading**

MONDAY, 16 MAY

9:00 AM – 10:40 AM

Total marks — 30

Attempt ALL questions.

Write your answers clearly, in **English**, in the Reading answer booklet provided. In the answer booklet you must clearly identify the question number you are attempting.

You may use a French dictionary.

Use **blue** or **black** ink.

There is a separate question and answer booklet for Directed Writing. You must complete your answer for Directed Writing in the question and answer booklet for Directed Writing.

Before leaving the examination room you must give your Reading answer booklet and your Directed Writing question and answer booklet to the Invigilator; if you do not, you may lose all the marks for this paper.

Total marks — 30

Attempt ALL questions

Read the whole article carefully and then answer, in **English**, ALL the questions that follow.

This article talks about an increasingly popular type of film which features young people as the main character.

L'adolescent, héros de cinéma

Jennifer Lawrence, star du film *Hunger Games*, est l'acteur du moment. Elle a déjà joué dans plusieurs films. Si on l'aime beaucoup, c'est peut-être parce qu'elle est différente des autres jeunes acteurs. Elle a grandi loin de New-York, dans l'état du Kentucky. Elle pratiquait des sports avec ses grands frères tout en étant majorette dans son lycée. Elle n'a jamais pris de
5   cours de théâtre et aucun de ses parents ne travaille dans le cinéma.

Jennifer n'est pas la seule star de cinéma sur nos écrans. Chaque semaine ou presque, des douzaines de nouveaux films avec des héros adolescents sortent au cinéma. Même si ce n'est pas un nouveau phénomène, il s'est développé massivement pendant les vingt dernières années, par exemple dans les films *Warhorse* et *Chronicle*. Pendant cette période le héros
10   typique est devenu de plus en plus jeune, ce qui attire une nouvelle clientèle également jeune.

Le nouveau héros typique

Ces films illustrent que les jeunes héros sont partout dans les films. Les directeurs de cinéma se sont inspirés des problèmes des jeunes tels que la drogue, l'amour et le stress des
15   examens. Cependant il faut avouer que les adolescents qui se disputent avec des adultes n'est pas du tout un nouveau thème au cinéma. Le héros typique de ce genre de films est souvent indépendant et parfois un peu rebelle. Il ou elle ne respecte plus aucune règle. Les parents, de leur côté, sont souvent absents. Ils sont incapables de leur donner des limites ou parfois même, ils abandonnent leur rôle de parents car leurs journées de travail sont de plus
20   en plus longues et épuisantes. Par conséquent, les adolescents sont souvent laissés seuls à la maison.

L'opinion des jeunes

Mais que pensent les jeunes de la façon dont le cinéma contemporain les représente? Ce qu'ils n'aiment pas, c'est l'image de l'adolescent malheureux, isolé, solitaire, l'adolescent qui
25   ne sait pas communiquer avec ses camarades de classe ou les adultes autour de lui et qui passe tout son temps devant son écran d'ordinateur.

Rémi Laporte, 17 ans, au lycée Pablo Picasso à Perpignan ajoute: «Je n'aime pas les comédies françaises qui montrent des images clichés des adolescents comme leur immaturité, leur colère, leur mauvaise humeur».

30   Selon l'expert David Martin, sociologue à l'Université de Nantes ce que les jeunes préfèrent, ce sont les films qui mettent en scène des bandes d'adolescents parfois effrontés qui font des bêtises ensemble, ou des bandes d'amis qui s'aident et essaient de résoudre leurs problèmes. Ils admettent cependant qu'ils les regardent avec une certaine distance car elles ne reflètent pas vraiment l'adolescence d'aujourd'hui.

35   ### La perte de l'innocence

Dans le monde occidental, ces films ont souvent pour intention de refléter la vie quotidienne des jeunes et en particulier les relations difficiles avec les parents est un thème que l'on trouve partout dans les films populaires. Au contraire dans les pays en développement, la présence d'adolescents dans les films sert plutôt à dénoncer la guerre, la pauvreté ou les
40   inégalités. En plus les films montrent comment, dans une grande partie du monde, on grandit trop vite et l'enfant devient adulte sans jamais être adolescent.

Pour les cinéastes, il est difficile de trouver le bon équilibre entre la réalité et le fantasme pour plaire au grand public.

Questions   MARKS

Re-read lines 1—5.

1. In what ways is Jennifer Lawrence different from other young actors? State any **three** things.   3

Re-read lines 6—11.

2. The writer discusses the increase in the number of films where the main character is a teenager.

   (a) What shows that this type of film is becoming more popular?   1

   (b) How has the typical main character changed over the last 20 years?   1

   (c) What effect has this had on cinema-going?   1

Re-read lines 16—21.

3. The writer goes on to discuss the typical main character in these films.

   (a) The writer states that the main character is often independent and rebellious. What else does the writer state about the main character?   1

   (b) (i) Parents are often absent from the main character's life. What examples demonstrate this?   2

       (ii) What is the result?   1

Re-read lines 22—34.

4. Young people do not always react positively to the way in which cinema portrays them.

   (a) They are often seen as unhappy, isolated and lonely. What other aspects of their portrayal do they not like?   2

   (b) Rémi does not like the way French comedies represent young people.

       Give an example of this.   1

   (c) According to the sociologist David Martin, what kind of films do young people like to watch? State any **two** things   2

[Questions 5 to 7 are on *Page four*

MARKS

Questions (continued)

Re-read lines 35—43

5. There are differences between the portrayal of young people in western and in developing countries.

    (a) What themes do films reflect **in western countries**? State any **one** thing.   **1**

    (b)   (i) What is the main theme of films **in developing countries**?   **1**

        (ii) What else do these films show? State any **one** thing.   **1**

6. Now consider the article as a whole.

    In what way do film makers represent young people in film? Give details from the text to justify your answer.   **2**

7. Translate into English the underlined section.

    «Ces films . . . au cinéma» (lines 13—16)   **10**

[END OF QUESTION PAPER]

FOR OFFICIAL USE

H

National Qualifications 2016

Mark ☐

X730/76/02

French Directed Writing

MONDAY, 16 MAY

9:00 AM – 10:40 AM

Fill in these boxes and read what is printed below.

Full name of centre

Town

Forename(s)

Surname

Number of seat

Date of birth

Day	Month	Year

Scottish candidate number

Total marks — 10

Choose ONE scenario on *Page two* and write your answer clearly, in **French**, in the space provided in this booklet. You must clearly identify the scenario number you are attempting.

You may use a French dictionary.

Additional space for answers is provided at the end of this booklet.

Use **blue** or **black** ink.

There is a separate answer booklet for Reading. You must complete your answers for Reading in the answer booklet for Reading.

Before leaving the examination room you must give this Directed Writing question and answer booklet and your Reading answer booklet to the Invigilator; if you do not, you may lose all the marks for this paper.

Total marks — 10

Choose **one** of the following two scenarios.

SCENARIO 1: Society

Last summer you had the opportunity to spend two months in the south of France. During your stay you travelled to other parts of France. On your return you have been asked to write an account **in French** of your experience for your school/college website.

You must include the following information and **you should try to add** other relevant details:

- why you went to France **and** what the journey was like
- what you thought of the areas you visited
- what you liked/disliked about the French way of life
- whether you would recommend this type of experience

You should write approximately 120—150 words.

OR

SCENARIO 2: Learning

Last year you went to France on an activities holiday with your school. During your stay you had the opportunity to try out some new sports and other activities. On your return you have been asked to write an account **in French** of your experience.

You must include the following information **and you should try to add** other relevant details:

- where exactly you went in France **and** who you went with
- what new sports or activities you took part in
- how you got on with the others taking part
- whether or not you would recommend this kind of holiday to others

You should write approximately 120—150 words.

ANSWER SPACE

MARKS | DO NOT WRITE IN THIS MARGIN

Scenario number

_____

_____

_____

_____

_____

_____

_____

_____

_____

_____

_____

_____

_____

_____

_____

_____

_____

_____

_____

_____

_____

_____

_____

[Turn over

MARKS

ANSWER SPACE (continued)

MARKS | DO NOT WRITE IN THIS MARGIN

ANSWER SPACE (continued)

_____

_____

_____

_____

_____

_____

_____

_____

_____

_____

_____

_____

_____

_____

_____

_____

_____

_____

_____

_____

_____

_____

[Turn over

MARKS | DO NOT WRITE IN THIS MARGIN

ANSWER SPACE (continued)

[END OF QUESTION PAPER]

MARKS | DO NOT WRITE IN THIS MARGIN

ADDITIONAL SPACE FOR ANSWERS

MARKS | DO NOT WRITE IN THIS MARGIN

ADDITIONAL SPACE FOR ANSWERS

FOR OFFICIAL USE

National
Qualifications
2016

Mark

X730/76/03

French
Listening and Writing

MONDAY, 16 MAY

11:00 AM – 12:00 NOON

Fill in these boxes and read what is printed below.

Full name of centre

Town

Forename(s)

Surname

Number of seat

Date of birth

Day	Month	Year		Scottish candidate number

Total marks — 30

SECTION 1 — LISTENING — 20 marks

You will hear two items in French. **Before you hear each item, you will have one minute to study the question.** You will hear each item twice, with an interval of one minute between playings. You will then have time to answer the questions before hearing the next item. Write your answers clearly, in **English**, in the spaces provided.

SECTION 2 — WRITING — 10 marks.

Write your answer clearly, in **French**, in the space provided.

Attempt ALL questions. You may use a French dictionary.

Additional space for answers is provided at the end of this booklet. If you use this space you must clearly identify the question number you are attempting.

You are not allowed to leave the examination room until the end of the test.

Use **blue** or **black** ink.

Before leaving the examination room you must give this booklet to the Invigilator; if you do not, you may lose all the marks for this paper.

MARKS | DO NOT WRITE IN THIS MARGIN

SECTION 1 — LISTENING — 20 marks

Attempt ALL questions

Item 1

Listen to this item about work placements in France.

(a) In what ways can work experience benefit a young person? State any **two** things.

2

_____

_____

(b) The reality of a job is often different. What kind of problems could you experience? State any **two** things.

2

_____

_____

(c) (i) What is the main benefit for the company?

1

_____

_____

(ii) What else can a young person bring to the company? State **two** things.

2

_____

_____

(d) Consider the report as a whole. Overall which statement best describes the report? Tick (✓) the correct statement.

1

	Tick (✓)
Work placements benefit an employer most	
Work placements benefit young people most	
Work placements benefit both employers and young people	

MARKS | DO NOT WRITE IN THIS MARGIN

Item 2

Carine and Pierre are discussing future plans.

(a) (i) What is Carine going to do first and why?

2

_____

_____

(ii) What exactly will she do during this year?

2

_____

_____

(b) (i) What are Carine's long term plans? State **two** things.

2

_____

_____

(ii) Why does she not want to go to university immediately? State any **two** things.

2

_____

_____

(c) In what ways did Carine benefit from working in hotels? State any **two** things.

2

_____

_____

(d) According to Carine what will be the positive aspects of her future career?

2

_____

_____

[Turn over

SECTION 2 — WRITING — 10 marks

Carine nous a parlé de ce qu'elle veut faire à l'avenir. Quelle sorte de métier est-ce que vous voulez faire à l'avenir? Quels sont les avantages et les inconvénients de prendre une année sabbatique?

Ecris 120—150 mots en français pour exprimer tes idées.

_____

_____

_____

_____

_____

_____

_____

_____

_____

_____

_____

_____

_____

_____

_____

_____

_____

_____

MARKS | DO NOT WRITE IN THIS MARGIN

ANSWER SPACE FOR SECTION 2 (continued)

[Turn over

MARKS DO NOT WRITE IN THIS MARGIN

ANSWER SPACE FOR SECTION 2 (continued)

[END OF QUESTION PAPER]

MARKS | DO NOT WRITE IN THIS MARGIN

ADDITIONAL SPACE FOR ANSWERS

Page seven

MARKS | DO NOT WRITE IN THIS MARGIN

ADDITIONAL SPACE FOR ANSWERS

National Qualifications 2016

X730/76/13

French
Listening Transcript

MONDAY, 16 MAY

11:00 AM – 12:00 NOON

This paper must not be seen by any candidate.

The material overleaf is provided for use in an emergency only (eg the recording or equipment proving faulty) or where permission has been given in advance by SQA for the material to be read to candidates with additional support needs. The material must be read exactly as printed.

Instructions to reader(s):

For each item, read the English **once**, then read the French **twice**, with an interval of 1 minute between the two readings. On completion of the second reading of Item Number One, pause for the length of time indicated in brackets after the item, to allow the candidates to write their answers.

Where special arrangements have been agreed in advance to allow the reading of the material, those sections marked **(f)** should be read by a female speaker and those marked **(m)** by a male; those sections marked **(t)** should be read by the teacher.

(t) **Item Number One**

Listen to this item about work placements in France.

You now have one minute to study the questions for Item Number One.

(f) Si vous voulez faire un stage en France il faut faire des recherches sur internet ou dans des magazines. Mais quels en sont les avantages pour les jeunes?

En effet, un stage peut avoir une grande importance pour tout le monde. Tout d'abord il vous permet de montrer aux futurs employeurs que vous avez non seulement de l'expérience dans le monde du travail mais aussi des compétences utiles pour votre carrière professionnelle. Enfin le stage peut vous permettre également de confirmer (ou non) votre intérêt pour une profession en particulier.

La réalité est souvent très différente. Par exemple on rencontre d'autres problèmes. Quelquefois on ne s'entend pas bien avec le patron. On doit commencer de bonne heure et parfois travailler de longues heures. L'avantage principal pour l'entreprise est que le stagiaire est moins payé qu'un employé permanent. De plus, un stagiaire peut partager de nouvelles idées ainsi que son enthousiasme avec ses collègues.

En conclusion on peut dire que le stage possède des avantages aussi bien pour l'étudiant que pour l'entreprise.

(2 minutes)

(t) Item Number Two

Carine and Pierre are discussing future plans.

You now have one minute to study the questions for Item Number Two.

(m) Au lycée on parle beaucoup de ce qu'on va faire à l'avenir. Tu as déjà pensé à ce que tu vas faire? Tu as des projets?

(f) Eh bien, en ce moment je ne sais pas exactement ce que je veux faire. Alors tout d'abord je crois que je vais prendre une année sabbatique. Je suis trop jeune pour choisir une carrière pour la vie.

(m) Alors, qu'est-ce que tu vas faire exactement pendant cette année?

(f) Je vais voyager autour du monde et en profiter pour découvrir de nouvelles cultures. De cette façon j'aurai quelque chose d'intéressant à dire quand je vais chercher un emploi plus tard.

(m) Qu'est-ce que tu as l'intention de faire après ton année sabbatique?

(f) A long terme, j'ai l'intention de travailler avec les enfants. Je vais peut-être faire des études pour devenir institutrice. C'est un métier qui m'attire parce que chaque jour est différent.

(m) Tu ne veux pas aller tout de suite à l'université?

(f) Non, je ne veux pas aller à la fac tout de suite. J'ai peur de faire un mauvais choix et je veux gagner un peu d'argent pour mettre de côté aussi. Comme ça j'aurai encore du temps pour décider quelles études je veux faire.

(m) Quelle sorte de travail est-ce que tu veux faire pendant ton année sabbatique?

(f) Ben, je n'en suis pas sûre. J'ai déjà travaillé comme serveuse et réceptionniste dans un hôtel près de chez moi. Je me suis très bien entendue avec mes collègues et en plus j'ai eu beaucoup de pourboires. A mon avis ce sont des boulots où l'on rencontre beaucoup de monde. J'aime beaucoup le contact avec le public.

(m) Ce n'était pas trop fatigant?

(f) Au contraire. J'ai trouvé que travailler à l'hôtel était un changement complet de ce que je devais faire au lycée. Là je pouvais oublier tout le stress du lycée et en même temps gagner de l'argent en m'amusant.

(m) Mais tu veux être institutrice? Travailler dans une école est dur quand même.

(f) Oui, je le sais, mais on a la satisfaction de voir les élèves faire des progrès. On a la responsabilité de l'avenir de ces jeunes personnes après tout.

(m) Oui, alors là tu as raison.

(t) End of recording.

[END OF TRANSCRIPT]

[BLANK PAGE]

DO NOT WRITE ON THIS PAGE

HIGHER

2017

National Qualifications 2017

X730/76/11

French Reading

MONDAY, 15 MAY

9:00 AM – 10:40 AM

Total marks — 30

Attempt ALL questions.

Write your answers clearly, in **English**, in the Reading answer booklet provided. In the answer booklet you must clearly identify the question number you are attempting.

You may use a French dictionary.

Use **blue** or **black** ink.

There is a separate question and answer booklet for Directed Writing. You must complete your answer for Directed Writing in the question and answer booklet for Directed Writing.

Before leaving the examination room you must give your Reading answer booklet and your Directed Writing question and answer booklet to the Invigilator; if you do not, you may lose all the marks for this paper.

Total marks — 30

Attempt ALL questions

Read the whole article carefully and then answer, in **English**, ALL the questions that follow.

The article discusses the importance of the media in France.

Les Français et les médias

En France, les médias jouent un rôle très important dans la vie quotidienne. Les Français écoutent la radio, lisent les journaux et regardent la télé. En effet, la télévision représente le premier loisir des Français qui avouent consacrer trois heures au minimum par jour au petit écran, c'est-à-dire cinquante minutes de plus que surfer sur Internet. La télévision reste
5 allumée même si personne ne la regarde! Les films, journaux télévisés et documentaires sont leurs programmes favoris.

Mais ce qui est inquiétant c'est que les programmes sont de moins bonne qualité et c'est pour ça que certains Français parlent de la «télé-réalité». Néanmoins ce genre d'émissions attire beaucoup de téléspectateurs. Jean-Marc, 20 ans, explique: «Après une longue journée
10 je veux tout simplement m'installer dans un fauteuil devant la télé pour m'éloigner du stress du travail. Voilà pourquoi je regarde beaucoup de télé-réalité. Pourtant je reconnais qu'il faut faire attention parce que ces émissions ne respectent pas la vie privée des gens et en plus elles n'ont rien à voir avec la vie du Français moyen.»

Par contre, il ne faut pas oublier que la télévision est un moyen efficace de s'informer de ce
15 qui se passe dans le monde. En seulement trente minutes les Français peuvent s'informer des événements importants dans le monde, tout en mangeant le repas du soir. Ils trouvent les actualités télévisées plus crédibles que les reportages dans la presse populaire. Les aspects positifs sont que les actualités télévisées sont très bien commentées et analysées. Les informations qui intéressent les Français concernent aussi bien les grands débats politiques à
20 l'approche des élections que les catastrophes naturelles même avec ses images brutales et effrayantes.

Les médias traditionnels menacés par Internet?

De nos jours, on a accès aux actualités à n'importe quelle heure de la journée. Les journaux et les magazines français sont moins menacés par Internet parce qu'ils possèdent maintenant
25 aussi leur propre site web. Ce sont surtout les jeunes qui ont tendance à accéder aux médias en ligne, et n'importe où. <u>Juliette Morelle qui prend le train tous les jours observe «On voit les jeunes partout taper sur leur tablette tout en regardant les émissions d'hier soir qu'ils ont téléchargées. Je dois dire que le bruit incessant m'énerve énormément.»</u> Toutefois un grand nombre de Français plus âgés continuent d'acheter leur journal quotidien dans les kiosques
30 ou bien même dans les supermarchés. Chose étonnante, la presse régionale reste le premier média national avec plus de 20 millions de lecteurs parce qu'elle s'intéresse, comme ses lecteurs, plus particulièrement aux événements du quartier. En outre, la presse gratuite est arrivée en 2002 et sa popularité continue d'augmenter et de rivaliser avec la presse payante.

La presse people

35 Soit en ligne, soit sur papier, le public reste fasciné par la vie des personnes célèbres. On voit tous les jours des articles qui racontent les moindres détails de la vie des stars. Les journalistes n'hésitent pas à publier des photos sans permission ni de raconter ce qu'ils mangent au petit déjeuner, avec qui ils sont sortis la semaine dernière. Mais il faut se demander à quoi ça sert et pourquoi les Français ont besoin de lire ce genre d'histoire.
40 Comme la télé-réalité, est-ce seulement un autre moyen d'échapper à la vie quotidienne?

MARKS

Questions

Re-read lines 1—13.

1. Television is the most popular form of media in France. In what ways does the writer highlight this?

3

2. People are watching more and more reality TV.

    (a) What is worrying about this trend?

1

    (b) Why is Jean-Marc attracted to this type of programme?

1

    (c) Which **two** negative aspects does Jean-Marc highlight in relation to these programmes?

2

Re-read lines 14—21.

3. Television news programmes are highly regarded in France.

    (a) In what ways are these programmes convenient for people?

2

    (b) What are the positive aspects of this type of programme?

1

    (c) What type of news reports are French people interested in? Give details.

2

Re-read lines 22—33.

4. The writer goes on to talk about the impact of the Internet on the media. Why are newspapers and magazines less threatened by the Internet?

1

5. According to the article, in what way do many older people access the news?

1

6. Why do regional newspapers still attract more than 20 million readers?

1

Re-read lines 34—40.

7. According to the article, celebrity magazines focus on the smallest details of celebrities' lives. What else does it say about these magazines?

3

MARKS

Questions (continued)

8.   Now consider the article as a whole.

     The article discusses how French people access and use the media. Does the writer think that the media play an important role in people's lives? Give reasons for your answer with reference to the text.   **2**

9.   Translate into English:

     "Juliette Morelle . . . énormément.»" (lines 26 to 28)   **10**

[END OF QUESTION PAPER]

[OPEN OUT]

DO NOT WRITE ON THIS PAGE

[BLANK PAGE]

DO NOT WRITE ON THIS PAGE

H

National Qualifications 2017

Mark

X730/76/02

French
Directed Writing

MONDAY, 15 MAY

9:00 AM – 10:40 AM

Fill in these boxes and read what is printed below.

Full name of centre

Town

Forename(s)

Surname

Number of seat

Date of birth

Day   Month   Year

Scottish candidate number

Total marks — 10

Choose ONE scenario on *Page two* and write your answer clearly, in **French**, in the space provided in this booklet. You must clearly identify the scenario number you are attempting.

You may use a French dictionary.

Additional space for answers is provided at the end of this booklet.

Use **blue** or **black** ink.

There is a separate answer booklet for Reading. You must complete your answers for Reading in the answer booklet for Reading.

Before leaving the examination room you must give this Directed Writing question and answer booklet and your Reading answer booklet to the Invigilator; if you do not, you may lose all the marks for this paper.

Total marks — 10

Choose **one** of the following two scenarios.

SCENARIO 1: Learning

> You recently took part in an exchange with your partner school in France. On your return you were asked to write an account **in French** of your experience for your school/college website.

You must include the following information and **you should try to add** other relevant details:

- where the school was located **and** what you thought of the school
- what you did to improve your French during your stay
- what benefits you gained from taking part in the school exchange
- whether or not you would recommend participating in a school exchange

You should write approximately 120—150 words.

OR

SCENARIO 2: Employability

> Last year you spent a month working in France. On your return you were asked to write an account **in French** of your experience for your school/college website.

You must include the following information and **you should try to add** other relevant details:

- who you went with **and** how you travelled
- what you had to do in your job
- what you did with the money you earned
- how your experience will benefit your future career

You should write approximately 120—150 words.

MARKS | DO NOT WRITE IN THIS MARGIN

ANSWER SPACE

Scenario number

_____

_____

_____

_____

_____

_____

_____

_____

_____

_____

_____

_____

_____

_____

_____

_____

_____

_____

_____

_____

_____

_____

_____

MARKS | DO NOT WRITE IN THIS MARGIN

ANSWER SPACE (continued)

MARKS | DO NOT WRITE IN THIS MARGIN

ANSWER SPACE (continued)

[Turn over

MARKS | DO NOT WRITE IN THIS MARGIN

ANSWER SPACE (continued)

[END OF QUESTION PAPER]

MARKS DO NOT WRITE IN THIS MARGIN

ADDITIONAL SPACE FOR ANSWERS

MARKS DO NOT WRITE IN THIS MARGIN

ADDITIONAL SPACE FOR ANSWERS

H

National Qualifications 2017

Mark ☐

X730/76/03

French
Listening and Writing

MONDAY, 15 MAY

11:00 AM – 12:00 NOON

Fill in these boxes and read what is printed below.

Full name of centre

Town

Forename(s)

Surname

Number of seat

Date of birth

Day	Month	Year

Scottish candidate number

Total marks — 30

SECTION 1 — LISTENING — 20 marks

You will hear two items in French. **Before you hear each item, you will have one minute to study the questions.** You will hear each item twice, with an interval of one minute between playings. You will then have time to answer the questions before hearing the next item. Write your answers clearly, in **English**, in the spaces provided.

SECTION 2 — WRITING — 10 marks

Write your answer clearly, in **French**, in the space provided.

You may use a French dictionary.

Additional space for answers is provided at the end of this booklet. If you use this space you must clearly identify the question number you are attempting.

Use **blue** or **black** ink.

You are not allowed to leave the examination room until the end of the test.

Before leaving the examination room you must give this booklet to the Invigilator; if you do not, you may lose all the marks for this paper.

MARKS | DO NOT WRITE IN THIS MARGIN

SECTION 1 — LISTENING — 20 marks

Attempt ALL questions

Item 1

You hear a radio report about holidays.

(a) What reasons do young people give for **not** wanting to spend holidays with their parents? State any **two**.

2

_____

_____

(b) It is normal for teenagers to want their independence. They also need their freedom. What else is important to them at this age? State **two** things.

2

_____

_____

(c) (i) Some parents are protective. What types of holidays are more suitable for their children? State any **one** thing.

1

_____

(ii) Give **one** example of how young people can benefit from these holidays.

1

_____

(d) Give **two** reasons why young people continue to go on holiday with their parents.

2

_____

_____

Item 2

MARKS | DO NOT WRITE IN THIS MARGIN

Pauline talks about her experience at a colonie de vacances, a summer camp for young people.

(a) Pauline first went to a colonie de vacances when she was 8 years old. Why did her parents send her there? State **two** things.   2

_____

_____

(b) (i) What type of activities did she do at the colonie de vacances? State **two** things.   2

_____

_____

    (ii) What was the aim of these activities? State any **one** thing.   1

_____

(c) Pauline grew in confidence at the colonie de vacances. What example does she give of this? State **two** things.   2

_____

_____

(d) She goes on to talk about a boy of the same age that she remembers.

    (i) He was very shy. What problems did the boy have? Give any **one** example.   1

_____

    (ii) What did Pauline do to help the boy? Give any **one** example.   1

_____

(e) Pauline is now working in a colonie de vacances. What does her job involve? State **two** things.   2

_____

_____

(f) This year she is going to a colonie de vacances near the Spanish border. Why will this be a good experience for her? State any **one** thing.   1

_____

MARKS | DO NOT WRITE IN THIS MARGIN

SECTION 2 — WRITING — 10 marks

Pauline nous a parlé de son expérience dans une colonie de vacances. Et toi, tu aimes les vacances organisées comme Pauline ou préfères-tu partir avec tes copains ou tes parents?

Ecris 120—150 mots en français pour exprimer tes idées.

MARKS DO NOT WRITE IN THIS MARGIN

ANSWER SPACE FOR SECTION 2 (continued)

MARKS | DO NOT WRITE IN THIS MARGIN

ANSWER SPACE FOR SECTION 2 (continued)

[END OF QUESTION PAPER]

ADDITIONAL SPACE FOR ANSWERS

MARKS | DO NOT WRITE IN THIS MARGIN

MARKS

ADDITIONAL SPACE FOR ANSWERS

National Qualifications 2017

X730/76/13

French
Listening Transcript

MONDAY, 15 MAY

11:00 AM – 12:00 NOON

This paper must not be seen by any candidate.

The material overleaf is provided for use in an emergency only (eg the recording or equipment proving faulty) or where permission has been given in advance by SQA for the material to be read to candidates with additional support needs. The material must be read exactly as printed.

Instructions to reader(s):

For each item, read the English **once**, then read the French **twice**, with an interval of 1 minute between the two readings. On completion of the second reading of Item Number One, pause for the length of time indicated in brackets after the item, to allow the candidates to write their answers.

Where special arrangements have been agreed in advance to allow the reading of the material, those sections marked **(f)** should be read by a female speaker and those marked **(m)** by a male; those sections marked **(t)** should be read by the teacher.

(t)   Item Number One

You hear a radio report about holidays.

You now have one minute to study the questions for Item Number One.

(f)   Pour beaucoup de familles, les vacances représentent le soleil, le repos, les loisirs. Mais, elles peuvent être aussi une source de disputes entre les parents et les adolescents. Les adolescents disent souvent «je ne suis plus un bébé», «les vacances en famille c'est ennuyeux», «mes copains me manquent».

Pour un adolescent il est normal de vouloir son indépendance. A cet âge, il a besoin de liberté, de prendre ses propres décisions, et de faire ses propres erreurs.

Si les parents sont protecteurs et inquiets, ils ne sont pas capables de laisser leur enfant partir tout seul avec ses copains. Ils préfèrent les vacances organisées, par exemple des séjours linguistiques ou des séjours en famille. Ce sont des options qui permettent aux jeunes de perfectionner une langue ou de découvrir une autre culture. S'il y a un problème il y a toujours un adulte à proximité.

Malgré tout cela, les jeunes aiment toujours partir en vacances avec les parents parce qu'ils se sentent en sécurité et en plus les parents paient tout: la nourriture, le logement et les activités. Finalement, partir en vacances en famille, ce n'est pas si mal après tout!

(2 minutes)

(t)   **Item Number Two**

Pauline talks about her experience at a colonie de vacances, a summer camp for young people.

You now have one minute to study the questions for Item Number Two.

(m)   Pauline, tu peux me parler de ton premier séjour en colonie de vacances?

(f)   Mon premier séjour dans une colonie de vacances était à l'âge de huit ans. J'étais un enfant très actif et j'aimais beaucoup être en plein air. Comme j'étais fille unique, je n'avais pas de frère et sœur pour jouer avec moi. Alors mes parents ont décidé de m'envoyer en colonie de vacances. Comme ça, j'étais moins seule.

(m)   Quelles sortes d'activités est-ce que tu as fait?

(f)   Pendant mon premier séjour j'ai fait beaucoup de choses, j'ai fait de la peinture et le soir j'ai joué à des jeux de société avec les autres enfants. Le but de ces activités était d'apprendre à jouer ensemble et à travailler en équipe.

(m)   Qu'est-ce que tu as appris en tant qu'enfant en colonie de vacances?

(f)   J'ai appris à être plus indépendante, et je trouve que je suis maintenant plus mûre. En plus, j'ai plus confiance en moi — par exemple j'ai aidé les plus jeunes quand ils avaient des problèmes, quand ils avaient le mal du pays ou quand leurs parents leur manquaient.

(m)   Tu te souviens d'une personne en particulier?

(f)   Oui, je me souviens d'un garçon du même âge que moi qui était très timide. Il ne parlait pas beaucoup et il ne voulait pas participer aux activités. J'ai passé beaucoup de temps avec lui, on a beaucoup parlé. Après trois ou quatre jours il est devenu moins réservé, plus bavard, plus sociable. A la fin des vacances il ne voulait pas rentrer chez lui. Cette expérience m'a encouragé à devenir animatrice moi-même.

(m)   Alors, maintenant que tu es animatrice dans une colonie de vacances, qu'est-ce que tu fais exactement comme travail?

(f)   Tous les soirs, il y a une réunion avec les collègues où l'on parle de l'emploi du temps pour le lendemain. Je dois aussi surveiller les enfants aux heures de repas.

(m)   Où vas-tu travailler cette année?

(f)   Pour la première fois je vais dans le sud de la France près de la frontière espagnole. C'est une région que je ne connais pas du tout. Alors, ce sera une bonne expérience pour moi. Et puisque cette année j'ai appris l'espagnol j'espère que je pourrai aller en Espagne pendant mes vacances.

(m)   Tu as de la chance Pauline. Amuse-toi bien!

(f)   Merci bien.

(t)   **End of recording.**

[END OF TRANSCRIPT]

[BLANK PAGE]

DO NOT WRITE ON THIS PAGE

HIGHER

2018

National Qualifications 2018

X730/76/11

French Reading

THURSDAY, 17 MAY
9:00 AM — 10:40 AM

Total marks — 30

Attempt ALL questions.

Write your answers clearly, in **English**, in the Reading answer booklet provided. In the answer booklet you must clearly identify the question number you are attempting.

You may use a French dictionary.

Use **blue** or **black** ink.

There is a separate question and answer booklet for Directed Writing. You must complete your answer for Directed Writing in the question and answer booklet for Directed Writing.

Before leaving the examination room you must give your Reading answer booklet and your Directed Writing question and answer booklet to the Invigilator; if you do not, you may lose all the marks for this paper.

Total marks — 30

Attempt ALL questions

Read the whole article carefully and then answer, in **English**, ALL the questions that follow.

This article talks about holidays in Madagascar, a French speaking island in the Indian Ocean.

Les vacances au paradis

Jean-Luc et sa fiancée Aline viennent de rentrer de l'île de Madagascar où ils ont passé quinze jours merveilleux. «Je n'hésiterais pas à recommander un tel séjour à ceux qui veulent s'éloigner des soucis du travail et se trouver hors des sentiers battus» dit Aline avec enthousiasme.

5   Située à neuf cents kilomètres de l'Afrique du Sud, Madagascar attire un grand nombre de touristes de tous les coins du monde. Il n'est pas difficile de voir pourquoi. Selon les guides touristiques, on peut s'attendre à être ému par l'accueil chaleureux qu'on recevra dès son arrivée.

En outre, il y a plein de choses à faire: se détendre avec un cocktail à la noix de coco sur les
10 belles plages de sable blanc ou visiter de nombreuses attractions naturelles et historiques pour ceux qui ne souhaitent pas passer tout leur temps à la plage. Au restaurant on peut aussi goûter de petits plats savoureux tels que le poisson à la mangue ou le riz légèrement épicé de gingembre. Cela a l'air d'être un véritable paradis!

Un début de vacances assez chaotique

15 Pourtant, ce n'est pas toujours le cas. Marc Bisset et Paul Bonneau, étudiants à l'université de Caen, sont allés à Madagascar l'été dernier. «On n'a pas pris contact avec un tour-opérateur parce que notre budget était trop serré. Il était moins cher de faire des recherches en ligne avant de partir pour savoir exactement ce que nous voulions voir et faire là-bas.»

«Une fois arrivés, après un vol de presque douze heures, on a vite découvert qu'il n'était pas
20 du tout facile de trouver une chambre si on n'avait pas réservé à l'avance. On a dû dormir sur la plage, mais on n'avait pas anticipé la présence de moustiques agaçants qui nous ont piqués toute la nuit. Les vacances commençaient mal!» a raconté Paul.

Après avoir passé quelques jours dans un petit village sur la côte, les deux étudiants ont décidé de louer une petite voiture afin d'explorer l'intérieur de cette île tropicale.

25 ### Vers l'intérieur

Marc et Paul ont quitté les plages ensoleillées de l'île pour explorer les montagnes magnifiques et les jolis petits villages nichés au cœur des forêts tropicales qui attirent les randonneurs ainsi que les photographes. Les deux étudiants ont aussi visité le parc d'*Andasibe Mantadia* connu pour ses espèces d'oiseaux rares et ses nombreuses variétés d'orchidées.

30 Marc explique: «Ce parc national est vraiment incontournable. On a la possibilité de faire des randonnées de différents niveaux dans la forêt et d'observer des lémuriens* en liberté. Bien que l'entrée ne soit pas gratuite, ça en vaut vraiment la peine. En plus, en achetant des tickets d'entrée, on participe à l'entretien de ce patrimoine naturel qui est actuellement en danger à cause de la déforestation.»

35 Le retour vers la côte n'a pas été facile. La nuit tombait quand les étudiants se sont trompés de route pendant un orage tropical et ils ont commencé à paniquer. Heureusement, après avoir parcouru quelques kilomètres, ils ont aperçu une petite maison où ils ont trouvé une famille hospitalière qui les a hébergés pour la nuit à l'abri de la pluie torrentielle. Il va sans dire que l'île de Madagascar est spectaculaire. A cause de cette expérience difficile, Marc et
40 Paul recommandent de faire toujours très attention aux conditions climatiques variables sur l'île pour éviter les problèmes. La prochaine fois ils seront mieux préparés.

*des lémuriens — lemurs (small animals native to Madagascar)

MARKS

Questions

Re-read lines 1—4.

1. According to Aline what kind of people would enjoy a holiday to Madagascar? State any **one** thing.

1

Re-read lines 9—13.

2. Madagascar has a lot to offer tourists. What can you do there? State **three** things.

3

Re-read lines 14—18.

3. Marc and Paul, students at the University of Caen, decided not to contact a tour operator before their trip.

   (a) What was their reason for this?

1

   (b)   (i) What did they decide to do instead?

1

         (ii) Why did they do this?

1

Re-read lines 19—22.

4. Marc and Paul's holiday did not get off to a good start. Why? State any **two** things.

2

Re-read lines 23—34.

5. They decided to visit the interior of the island.

   (a) Apart from the magnificent mountains what else is there to discover?

1

   (b) The students also went to the *Andasibe Mantadia* national park. What is the park famous for? State **two** things.

2

   (c) Marc says that the park is an experience not to be missed.

       (i) Why? State **two** details.

2

       (ii) Why does he think it is important to charge tourists an entry fee?

1

MARKS

Questions (continued)

Re-read lines 35—41.

6. The students' journey back to the coast was challenging. What happened to them on the way? Give any **three** details.

3

Now consider the article as a whole.

7. Would the writer recommend a holiday in Madagascar? Give details from the text to justify your answer.

2

8. Translate into English:

Située à . . . son arrivée. (lines 5—8)

10

[END OF QUESTION PAPER]

Page five

[OPEN OUT]

DO NOT WRITE ON THIS PAGE

[BLANK PAGE]

DO NOT WRITE ON THIS PAGE

H

National Qualifications 2018

Mark

X730/76/02

French
Directed Writing

THURSDAY, 17 MAY
9:00 AM — 10:40 AM

Fill in these boxes and read what is printed below.

Full name of centre

Town

Forename(s)

Surname

Number of seat

Date of birth

Day   Month   Year

Scottish candidate number

Total marks — 10

Choose ONE scenario on *Page two* and write your answer clearly, in **French**, in the space provided in this booklet. You must clearly identify the scenario number you are attempting.

You may use a French dictionary.

Additional space for answers is provided at the end of this booklet.

Use **blue** or **black** ink.

There is a separate answer booklet for Reading. You must complete your answers for Reading in the answer booklet for Reading.

Before leaving the examination room you must give this Directed Writing question and answer booklet and your Reading answer booklet to the Invigilator; if you do not, you may lose all the marks for this paper.

Total marks — 10

Choose **one** from the following two scenarios.

SCENARIO 1: Society

> Your school/college has organised an exchange trip to France. As part of the programme, you spend several days staying with a French family. On your return you are asked to write an account of your experience **in French** for your school/college website.

You must include the following information and **you should try to add** other relevant details:

- who you went with **and** how you travelled
- what the family's house was like
- what activities the family organised for you
- whether or not you would recommend doing a similar exchange

You should write approximately 120—150 words.

OR

SCENARIO 2: Learning

> You get the chance to take part in a two week language course in France during the summer. On your return you are asked to write an account of your experience **in French** for the school/college website.

You must include the following information and **you should try to add** other relevant details:

- where you stayed **and** what you thought of the area
- what you did during the day on the course
- what activities you did in the evening
- how you think you will benefit from your experience in the future

You should write approximately 120—150 words.

MARKS | DO NOT WRITE IN THIS MARGIN

ANSWER SPACE

Scenario number [   ]

_____

_____

_____

_____

_____

_____

_____

_____

_____

_____

_____

_____

_____

_____

_____

_____

_____

_____

_____

_____

_____

_____

ANSWER SPACE (continued)

ANSWER SPACE (continued)

MARKS | DO NOT WRITE IN THIS MARGIN

ANSWER SPACE (continued)

[END OF QUESTION PAPER]

MARKS | DO NOT WRITE IN THIS MARGIN

ADDITIONAL SPACE FOR ANSWERS

MARKS | DO NOT WRITE IN THIS MARGIN

ADDITIONAL SPACE FOR ANSWERS

H

National Qualifications 2018

Mark

X730/76/03

French
Listening and Writing

THURSDAY, 17 MAY

11:00 AM – 12:00 NOON

Fill in these boxes and read what is printed below.

Full name of centre

Town

Forename(s)

Surname

Number of seat

Date of birth

Day	Month	Year	Scottish candidate number

Total marks — 30

SECTION 1 — LISTENING — 20 marks

You will hear two items in French. **Before you hear each item, you will have one minute to study the questions.** You will hear each item twice, with an interval of one minute between playings. You will then have time to answer the questions before hearing the next item. Write your answers clearly, in **English**, in the spaces provided.

SECTION 2 — WRITING — 10 marks

Write your answer clearly, in **French**, in the space provided.

You may use a French dictionary.

Additional space for answers is provided at the end of this booklet. If you use this space you must clearly identify the question number you are attempting.

Use **blue** or **black** ink.

You are not allowed to leave the examination room until the end of the test.

Before leaving the examination room you must give this booklet to the Invigilator; if you do not, you may lose all the marks for this paper.

MARKS | DO NOT WRITE IN THIS MARGIN

SECTION 1 — LISTENING — 20 marks

Attempt ALL questions

Item 1

Vincent, a student, talks about interview techniques.

(a) How long does an interview usually last?

1

_____

(b) According to Vincent, what must you have with you on the day of the interview? State **two** things.

2

_____

_____

(c) What should you talk about during the interview? State **two** things.

2

_____

_____

(d) What will the employer ask you questions about? State any **two** things.

2

_____

_____

(e) What does Vincent recommend you do at the end of the interview?

1

_____

_____

Item 2

Séverine is discussing recent job interviews with Antoine.

(a) Where did she work last year?

1

_____

(b) Séverine's interview gets off to a bad start. What does she say? State any **two** things.

2

_____

_____

(c) Séverine was embarrassed during the interview. Why? State **two** things.

2

_____

_____

_____

(d) She also panicked during the interview. What happened as a result of this?

2

_____

_____

(e) Séverine is positive about her next interview for a job selling ice cream. Why is this?

1

_____

_____

(f) Apart from the good weather and the working hours, what are the other positive aspects of this job? State **two** things.

2

_____

_____

(g) If Séverine is successful she will go to work by bike. What are the advantages of this? State any **two** things.

2

_____

_____

MARKS | DO NOT WRITE IN THIS MARGIN

SECTION 2 — WRITING — 10 marks

Séverine a discuté de ses entretiens et des jobs d'été. Et toi, est-ce que tu veux un petit boulot? Pourquoi? Quels sont les avantages de gagner de l'argent?

Ecris 120—150 mots en français pour exprimer tes idées.

MARKS DO NOT WRITE IN THIS MARGIN

ANSWER SPACE FOR SECTION 2 (continued)

[Turn over

ANSWER SPACE FOR SECTION 2 (continued)

[END OF QUESTION PAPER]

MARKS | DO NOT WRITE IN THIS MARGIN

ADDITIONAL SPACE FOR ANSWERS

ADDITIONAL SPACE FOR ANSWERS

National Qualifications 2018

X730/76/13

**French
Listening Transcript**

THURSDAY, 17 MAY

11:00 AM – 12:00 NOON

This paper must not be seen by any candidate.

The material overleaf is provided for use in an emergency only (eg the recording or equipment proving faulty) or where permission has been given in advance by SQA for the material to be read to candidates with additional support needs. The material must be read exactly as printed.

Instructions to reader(s):

For each item, read the English **once**, then read the French **twice**, with an interval of 1 minute between the two readings. On completion of the second reading of Item Number One, pause for the length of time indicated in brackets after the item, to allow the candidates to write their answers.

Where special arrangements have been agreed in advance to allow the reading of the material, those sections marked **(f)** should be read by a female speaker and those marked **(m)** by a male; those sections marked **(t)** should be read by the teacher.

(t)   Item Number One

Vincent, a student, talks about interview techniques.

You now have one minute to study the questions for Item Number One.

(m) Un premier entretien d'embauche dure en général entre 30 minutes et une heure. Il se passe souvent dans un bureau avec un employeur et quelquefois un ou deux autres collègues. Voici quelques conseils pour éviter le stress. Le jour de l'entretien il faut absolument avoir le numéro de téléphone de l'entreprise et le nom de la personne que vous allez rencontrer si vous avez un problème.

Pendant l'entretien vous devez parler des points importants de votre CV et expliquer pourquoi vous postulez pour ce poste. Il est très important de préparer cette présentation avec un ami avant l'entretien. Je vous conseille de faire des recherches concernant l'entreprise sur Internet par exemple. L'employeur va vous poser des questions plus personnelles sur vos compétences et vos expériences précédentes. Il peut aussi vous demander de parler des responsabilités que vous avez eues dans un autre boulot. À la fin de l'entretien je vous recommande de poser des questions sur les conditions de travail même si ce n'est pas obligatoire.

(2 minutes)

(t)   Item Number Two

Séverine is discussing recent job interviews with Antoine.

You now have one minute to study the questions for Item Number Two.

(m) Alors Séverine qu'est-ce que tu voudrais faire comme boulot cet été?

(f) Je voudrais changer un peu cette année parce que l'été dernier j'ai travaillé dans la boulangerie de mon village. Mais cette année je voudrais travailler en plein air. J'ai eu un entretien cette semaine pour travailler comme plagiste à Cannes. Mais l'entretien n'a pas été très positif.

(m) Ah bon; et pourquoi? Qu'est-ce qu'il s'est passé?

(f) C'était une véritable catastrophe. Il y avait un accident de voiture, la route était fermée et, par conséquent, je suis arrivée quinze minutes en retard. Je pense que j'ai donné une très mauvaise impression de moi.

(m) Et comment s'est passé l'entretien?

(f) Ne m'en parle pas! C'était trop embarrassant. Je me suis présentée en vêtements de sport parce que c'était pour un poste sur la plage. Par contre les employeurs portaient un costume et je n'étais pas du tout habillée comme eux. En plus, pendant l'entretien mon téléphone a sonné deux fois car j'avais oublié de l'éteindre en arrivant dans le bureau. Je voulais disparaître!

(m) Ah oui, en effet c'est dommage! Comment as-tu répondu aux questions?

(f) Avec cette situation désastreuse j'ai paniqué. Tout d'abord je ne savais pas comment répondre aux questions et, en plus, mes réponses étaient trop courtes. Mais j'ai un entretien jeudi prochain pour un autre boulot.

(m) Génial. C'est pour quelle sorte de boulot?

(f) C'est pour être vendeuse de glaces sur la plage pour juillet et août. Je suis positive car ma copine va m'aider à préparer l'entretien.

(m) Quelle chance de travailler sur la plage!

(f) Ben oui. À Cannes il fait toujours beau et chaud. Les horaires me conviennent car je commencerai à 11h00 et je finirai à 20h00 donc je pourrai dormir le matin. Ma copine dit que les gens sont détendus quand ils sont en vacances. Et puis tu me connais . . . j'adore les glaces donc je pourrai en manger tant que je veux.

(m) Ce serait bien ce boulot mais tu n'habites pas à Cannes. Comment feras-tu pour y aller?

(f) Ça, c'est le problème car c'est à 10 kilomètres. Heureusement, j'ai mon vélo donc je pourrai circuler plus facilement en ville et éviter les embouteillages. Avec toutes les glaces que je mangerai je devrai faire un effort pour rester en forme!

(t)   End of recording.

[END OF TRANSCRIPT]

[BLANK PAGE]

DO NOT WRITE ON THIS PAGE

HIGHER

Answers

HIGHER FRENCH 2016

Reading

Question			Expected response(s)	Max mark
1.			• She grew up far from New York/in (the state of) Kentucky • She did sport(s) with her (older) brother(s), <u>while being a cheerleader/majorette</u> • She has never/not taken drama/acting/theatre class(es)/lesson(s)/course(s) • Neither of her parents/her parents don't work in (the) (world of) cinema/film industry *Any three of above 4 points for 3 marks*	3
2.	(a)		• (Almost) <u>every/each week</u>, dozens/lots of new films with teenage/young lead actors/heroes/main characters/protagonists are released/come out/appear (in the cinema/in cinema)	1
	(b)		• The (lead) actor(s)/(main) character(s)/protagonist(s)/(typical) hero(es)/they/he/she is/are becoming <u>younger and younger/more and more young</u>	1
	(c)		• It attracts a (new) <u>young</u> audience/an audience of youth/group(s) of <u>young</u> people/customers/clients/clientele OR • It attracts people who are equally young/of a similar age (to the main characters)/who are also teenagers/cinema goers are becoming younger also *Any one of above 2 points for 1 mark*	1
3.	(a)		• He/she/it doesn't/they don't respect/ follow/disrespect(s) any/the/all of the rules (any more)	1
	(b)	(i)	• Incapable of giving/setting/making/establishing/putting limits/boundaries/parameters/rules Not able to/can't give/set/make/establish/put limits/boundaries/parameters/rules • (Often) abandon/give up their role/duty/duties (as parents)	2
		(ii)	• The teenagers/children/kids/they are (often) (left) <u>alone/by themselves at home/in the house/home alone</u>	1

Question			Expected response(s)	Max mark
4.	(a)		• Teenagers do not know how to/can't/are unable to communicate with/speak/talk to peers/classmates/friends <u>and/or</u> adults/grown-ups (around them) • They spend/pass <u>all</u> (of) their/the time in front of/on/behind their computer (screen)/laptop	2
	(b)		• They are/he/she is shown as immature/angry/bad tempered/moody OR • It shows/they show their immaturity/anger/bad temper *Any one of above 2 points for 1 mark*	1
	(c)		• (Films that feature/show/films with) <u>groups/gangs/crowds/hordes/a lot of</u> young people/teenagers/friends/pals/mates/buddies (together) *plus one of the following* • who are (sometimes) cheeky/insolent/impudent • who muck about/get up to mischief/do silly/stupid things/being silly/stupid • who help <u>one another/each other</u> • try to solve <u>their/each other's</u> problems *Idea of groups plus one additional detail = 2 marks*	2
5.	(a)		• The <u>daily/everyday</u> life (of young people) OR • Difficult/trying relationship(s)/relations/difficulty(ies) (getting along) with parents/difficultly(ies) between teens and parents *Any one of above 2 points for 1 mark*	1
	(b)	(i)	• Denouncing/condemning/arguing against/opposing/fighting (against)/showing/portraying/exposing/talking about/reporting on/highlighting war/poverty/inequality *NB: need verb plus one detail for 1 mark*	1
		(ii)	• They/one/you/we/children/people/teenagers grow up <u>too fast/quickly/soon/early</u> • They/one/you/we/children/people become adult without (ever) experiencing adolescence/being a teenager/teen *Any one of above 2 points for 1 mark*	1

Question			Expected response(s)	Max mark
6.			*Assertion + justification in English = 2 marks*	2
			Outline of possible response and evidence:	
			Young people are shown negatively/ in a bad/pessimistic light/ as troubled/as problematic/as stereotypes/as clichés	
			• image of teenager who cannot communicate	
			• who spend all their time in front of a computer	
			• rebellious/disrespect rules	
			• product of poor parenting	
			• isolated/unhappy/alone	
			• any other negative detail from the text	
			OR	
			Young people are shown positively/ in a good/optimistic light/as kind/ as helpful	
			• groups of friends who help each other solving their problems	
			• interested in world issues/war/ poverty/inequality	
			• any other positive detail from the text	
			OR	
			Young people are shown in both a positive and negative/neutral light	
			• any one positive detail <u>and</u> any one negative detail from above	
			OR	
			Young people in western and developing countries are represented differently	
			In western countries:	
			• difficulties with parents	
			• daily life	
			In developing countries:	
			• teenagers denouncing war/ poverty/inequality	
			• they grow up too quickly	
			NB: any one detail from western countries <u>and</u> one detail from developing countries	

Question 7 – Translation

The translation into English is allocated 10 marks. The text for translation will be divided into a number of sense units. Each sense unit is worth 2 marks, which will be awarded according to the quality and accuracy of the translation into English.

1	*2 marks available:*
Ces films illustrent que les jeunes héros sont partout dans les films.	**These films illustrate/ show that young heroes are everywhere in films.**
Ces films	These/those films/movies
illustrent que	illustrate/show/demonstrate (that/how)
les jeunes héros	young heroes
sont partout dans les films.	are everywhere in films/movies in the films/movies in film.

2	*2 marks available:*
Les directeurs de cinéma se sont inspirés des problèmes des jeunes	**Film directors are inspired by young people's problems**
Les directeurs de cinéma	(The) (film/cinema) directors (The) directors of cinema
se sont inspirés	are inspired by take inspiration from
des problèmes des jeunes	young people's problems the problems of young people the problems young people have/face

3	*2 marks available:*
tels que la drogue, l'amour et le stress des examens.	**such as drugs, love and exam stress.**
tels que	such as like
la drogue, l'amour et le stress des examens.	drugs, love and exam stress/ the stress of exams.

4	*2 marks available:*
Cependant il faut avouer que les adolescents qui se disputent avec des adultes	**However, you have to admit that teenagers arguing with adults**
Cependant	However/but/nevertheless
il faut avouer que	you/one/we have to/must/ need to/got to admit/confess (that) it must be admitted/confessed (that)
les adolescents qui se disputent avec des adultes	teenagers/adolescents arguing/fighting/quarrelling with/who argue/fight/quarrel/ have disputes with adults

5	*2 marks available:*
n'est pas du tout un nouveau thème au cinéma.	**is not at all a new theme in film.**
n'est pas du tout	is not at all is not in any way
un nouveau thème au cinéma.	a new theme in film/(the) cinema/movies/film industry a new cinematic theme.

Directed Writing

Candidates will write a piece of extended writing in French addressing a scenario that has four related bullet points. Candidates must address each bullet point. The first bullet point contains two pieces of information to be addressed. The remaining three bullet points contain one piece of information each. There is a choice of two scenarios and learners must choose one of these.

Mark	Content	Accuracy	Language resource: variety, range, structures
10	• The content is comprehensive • All bullet points are addressed fully and some candidates may also provide additional relevant information	• The language is accurate in all four bullets. However, where the candidate attempts to go beyond the range of the task, a slightly higher number of inaccuracies need not detract from the overall very good impression • A comprehensive range of verbs is used accurately and tenses are consistent and accurate • There is evidence of confident handling of all aspects of grammar and accurate spelling, although the language may contain a number of minor errors, or even one serious error • Where the candidate attempts to go beyond the range of the task, a slightly higher number of inaccuracies need not detract from the overall very good impression	• The language used is detailed and complex • There is good use of adjectives, adverbs, prepositional phrases and, where appropriate, word order • A comprehensive range of verbs/verb forms, tenses and constructions is used • Some modal verbs and infinitives may be used • The candidate is comfortable with the first person of the verb and generally uses a different verb in each sentence • Sentences are mainly complex and accurate • The language flows well
8	• The content is clear • All bullet points are addressed clearly. The response to one bullet point may be thin, although other bullet points are dealt with in some detail	• The language is mostly accurate. Where the candidate attempts to use detailed and complex language, this may be less successful, although basic structures are used accurately • A range of verbs is used accurately and tenses are generally consistent and accurate • There may be a few errors in spelling, adjective endings and, where relevant, case endings. Use of accents is less secure, where relevant	• The language used is detailed and complex • In one bullet point the language may be more basic than might otherwise be expected at this level • The candidate uses a range of verbs/verb forms and other constructions • There may be less variety in the verbs used • The candidate is comfortable with the first person of the verb and generally uses a different verb in each sentence • Sentences are generally complex and mainly accurate • Overall the writing will be very competent, essentially correct, but may be pedestrian

Mark	Content	Accuracy	Language resource: variety, range, structures
6	• The content is adequate and may be similar to that of an 8 • Bullet points may be addressed adequately, however one of the bullet points may not be addressed	• The language may be mostly accurate in two or three bullet points. However, in the remaining one or two, control of the language structure may deteriorate significantly • The verbs are generally correct, but basic • Tenses may be inconsistent, with present tenses being used at times instead of past tenses • There may be errors in spelling, adjective endings and some prepositions may be inaccurate or omitted. There are quite a few errors in other parts of speech – personal pronouns, gender of nouns, adjective endings, cases (where relevant), singular/plural confusion – and in the use of accents (where relevant) • Overall, there is more correct than incorrect and there is the impression that the candidate can handle tenses	• There are some examples of detailed and complex language • The language is perhaps repetitive and uses a limited range of verbs and fixed phrases not appropriate to this level • The candidate relies on a limited range of vocabulary and structures • There is minimal use of adjectives, probably mainly after "is" • The candidate has a limited knowledge of plurals • A limited range of verbs is used to address some of the bullet points • The candidate copes with the past tense of some verbs • When using the perfect tense, the past participle is incorrect or the auxiliary verb is omitted on occasion • Sentences are mainly single clause and may be brief
4	• The content may be limited and the Directed Writing may be presented as a single paragraph • Bullet points may be addressed in a limited way or • **Two** of the bullet points are not be addressed	• The language is mainly inaccurate and after the first bullet the control of the language structure may deteriorate significantly • A limited range of verbs is used • Ability to form tenses is inconsistent • In the use of the perfect tense the auxiliary verb is omitted on a number of occasions • There may be confusion between the singular and plural form of verbs • There are errors in many other parts of speech – gender of nouns, cases, singular/plural confusion – and in spelling and, where appropriate, word order • Several errors are serious, perhaps showing mother tongue interference	• There is limited use of detailed and complex language • The language is repetitive, with undue reliance on fixed phrases and a limited range of common basic verbs such as to be, to have, to play, to watch • The candidate mainly copes only with simple language • The verbs "was" and "went" may also be used correctly • Sentences are basic and there may be one sentence that is not intelligible to a sympathetic native speaker • An English word may appear in the writing or a word may be omitted • There may be an example of serious dictionary misuse
2	• The content may be basic or similar to that of a 4 or even a 6 • Bullet points are addressed with difficulty	• The language is inaccurate in all four bullets and there is little control of language structure • Many of the verbs are incorrect or even omitted. There is little evidence of tense control • There are many errors in other parts of speech — personal pronouns, gender of nouns, cases, singular/plural confusion, prepositions, for instance	• There is little use, if any, of detailed and complex language • Verbs used more than once may be written differently on each occasion • The candidate displays almost no knowledge of the past tense of verbs • The candidate cannot cope with more than one or two basic verbs • Sentences are very short and some sentences may not be understood by a sympathetic native speaker
0	• The content is very basic • The candidate is unable to address the bullet points Or • **Three** or more of the bullet points are not addressed	• The language is seriously inaccurate in all four bullets and there is almost no control of language structure • Most errors are serious • Virtually nothing is correct • Very little is intelligible to a sympathetic native speaker	• There is no evidence of detailed and complex language • The candidate may only cope with the verbs to have and to be • There may be several examples of mother tongue interference • English words are used • Very few words are written correctly in the modern language • There may be several examples of serious dictionary misuse

Section 1 — Listening

Item 1

Question			Expected response(s)	Max mark
1.	(a)		• You gain experience of the world of work • You gain/develop/have useful skills/necessary skills/useful competence • It confirms whether or not you are interested in a particular job/confirms what you would like to do/whether you want to do the job or not (candidate must convey idea of interest in the job) *Any two of above 3 points for 2 marks*	2
	(b)		• You do not get on with/do not have a good relationship with the manager/boss • You have to start/begin/commence early • You have to work long hours/shifts *NB: start early and finish late = 2 marks* *Any two of above 3 points for 2 marks*	2
	(c)	(i)	• (The person on work experience) is paid less/isn't paid as much/gets lower wages/it's cheaper	1
		(ii)	• New/fresh ideas/perspectives • Enthusiasm/they are enthusiastic	2
	(d)		• Work placements benefit both employers and young people (last box)	1

Section 2 — Writing

Candidates will write 120—150 words in a piece of extended writing in French addressing a stimulus of three questions in French.

Item 2

Question			Expected response(s)	Max mark
2.	(a)	(i)	• Take a gap year/a year off/sabbatical year/year abroad • She is (too) young/not old enough to choose/decide on a career for life/future career *NB: there must be the idea of not knowing what career to choose*	2
		(ii)	• Travel (around) the world • (Benefit from) discovering/seeing/experiencing new culture(s)	2
	(b)	(i)	• She wants to work with children • Become a primary teacher *NB: Teach children = 1 mark*	2
		(ii)	• She is scared of making/she does not want to make a bad/wrong choice/decision • She wants to earn/make/save money (to put aside for university) • She wants (time) to decide which course/subjects she wants to study/doesn't know which subjects to do/doesn't know what to study *Any two of above 3 points for 2 marks*	2
	(c)		• She got on well with her colleagues/other staff • She got lots of tips • She could meet lots of people/likes the contact with the public • Complete/total change from school • Forgot/got away from the stress of school • Earned money at the same time as/while having fun/enjoying herself *Any two of above 6 points for 2 marks*	2
	(d)		• The satisfaction of seeing pupils/children/students making progress • The fact that she is responsible for their future/plays a part in shaping their future	2

Mark	Content	Accuracy	Language resource: variety, range, structures
10	• The content is comprehensive • The topic is addressed fully, in a balanced way • Some candidates may also provide additional information • Overall this comes over as a competent, well thought-out response to the task which reads naturally	• The language is accurate throughout. However where the candidate attempts to go beyond the range of the task, a slightly higher number of inaccuracies need not detract from the overall very good impression • A comprehensive range of verbs is used accurately and tenses are consistent and accurate • There is evidence of confident handling of all aspects of grammar and spelling accurately, although the language may contain a number of minor errors, or even one serious major error	• The language used is detailed and complex • There is good use of adjectives, adverbs, prepositional phrases and, where appropriate, word order • A comprehensive range of verbs/verb forms, tenses and constructions is used • Some modal verbs and infinitives may be used • The candidate is comfortable with the first person of the verb and generally uses a different verb in each sentence • The candidate uses co-ordinating conjunctions and subordinate clauses throughout the writing • Sentences are mainly complex and accurate • The language flows well

Mark	Content	Accuracy	Language resource: variety, range, structures
8	• The content is clear • The topic is addressed clearly	• The language is mostly accurate. However where the candidate attempts to use detailed and complex language, this may be less successful, although basic structures are used accurately • A range of verbs is used accurately and tenses are generally consistent and accurate • There may be a few errors in spelling, adjective endings and, where relevant, case endings. Use of accents is less secure • Verbs and other parts of speech are used accurately but simply	• The language used is detailed and complex • The candidate uses a range of verbs/verb forms and other constructions • There may be less variety in the verbs used • The candidate is comfortable with the first person of the verb and generally uses a different verb in each sentence • Most of the more complex sentences use co-ordinating conjunctions, and there may also be examples of subordinating conjunctions where appropriate • Sentences are generally complex and mainly accurate • At times the language may be more basic than might otherwise be expected at this level • There may be an example of minor misuse of dictionary • Overall the writing will be very competent, essentially correct, but may be pedestrian
6	• The content is adequate and may be similar to that of an 8 or a 10 • The topic is addressed adequately	• The language may be mostly accurate. However, in places, control of the language structure may deteriorate significantly • The verbs are generally correct, but basic. Tenses may be inconsistent, with present tenses being used at times instead of past tenses • There may be errors in spelling, e.g. reversal of vowel combinations adjective endings and some prepositions may be inaccurate or omitted, e.g. I went the town. There are quite a few errors in other parts of speech – personal pronouns, gender of nouns, adjective endings, cases, singular/plural confusion – and in the use of accents • Overall, there is more correct than incorrect and there is the impression that the candidate can handle tenses	• There are some examples of detailed and complex language • The language is perhaps repetitive and uses a limited range of verbs and fixed phrases not appropriate to this level • The candidate relies on a limited range of vocabulary and structures • There is minimal use of adjectives, probably mainly after "is" • The candidate has a limited knowledge of plurals • The candidate copes with the present tense of most verbs • Where the candidate attempts constructions with modal verbs, these are not always successful • Sentences are mainly single clause and may be brief • There may be some misuse of dictionary

Mark	Content	Accuracy	Language resource: variety, range, structures
4	• The content may be limited and may be presented as a single paragraph • The topic is addressed in a limited way	• The language used to address the more predictable aspects of the task may be accurate. However, major errors occur when the candidate attempts to address a less predictable aspect • A limited range of verbs is used • Ability to form tenses is inconsistent • In the use of the perfect tense the auxiliary verb is omitted on a number of occasions • There may be confusion between the singular and plural form of verbs • There are errors in many other parts of speech – gender of nouns, cases, singular/plural confusion – and in spelling and, where appropriate, word order • Several errors are serious, perhaps showing mother tongue interference • Overall there is more incorrect than correct	• There is limited use of detailed and complex language and the language is mainly simple and predictable • The language is repetitive, with undue reliance on fixed phrases and a limited range of common basic verbs such as to be, to have, to play, to watch • There is inconsistency in the use of various expressions, especially verbs • Sentences are basic and there may be one sentence that is not intelligible to a sympathetic native speaker • An English word may appear in the writing or a word may be omitted • There may be an example of serious dictionary misuse
2	• The content may be basic or similar to that of a 4 or even a 6 • The topic is thinly addressed	• The language is almost completely inaccurate throughout the writing and there is little control of language structure • Many of the verbs are incorrect or even omitted. There is little evidence of tense control • There are many errors in other parts of speech — personal pronouns, gender of nouns, cases, singular/plural confusion • Prepositions are not used correctly	• There is little use, if any, of detailed and complex language • The candidate has a very limited vocabulary • Verbs used more than once may be written differently on each occasion • The candidate cannot cope with more than one or two basic verbs • Sentences are very short and some sentences may not be understood by a sympathetic native speaker • Several English or "made-up" words may appear in the writing • There are examples of serious dictionary misuse
0	• The content is very basic • The candidate is unable to address the topic	• The language is seriously inaccurate throughout the writing and there is almost no control of language structure • (Virtually) nothing is correct • Most of the errors are serious • Very little is intelligible to a sympathetic native speaker	• There is no evidence of detailed and complex language • The candidate copes only with "have" and "am" • There may be several examples of mother tongue interference • Very few words are written correctly in the modern language • English words are used • There may be several examples of serious dictionary misuse

HIGHER FRENCH 2017

Reading

Question			Expected response(s)	Max mark
1.			• They <u>watch</u> (television) <u>at least/minimum three</u> hours <u>a day</u> • This is 50 minutes <u>more than</u> surfing the net/going online • The TV is on even if <u>no-one/nobody is/people</u> are not watching it	3
2.	(a)		• The programmes are of <u>less</u> good quality/less/not <u>as</u> good/low<u>er</u>/poor<u>er</u>/worse <u>quality</u> OR • Programmes have reduced in (good) <u>quality</u> *Any one of above 2 points for 1 mark*	1
	(b)		• To get away/distance/move away from/escape/detach <u>yourself</u>/remove <u>yourself</u> from the stress of <u>work</u>	1
	(c)		• They don't respect people's <u>private/personal</u> life/lives OR • Your privacy is not respected • They have nothing to do with/are nothing like the <u>average</u> French <u>person's</u> life/nothing like the lives of an <u>average</u> French <u>person</u>	2
3.	(a)		• They/it <u>only</u> last(s) 30 minutes/<u>no more than</u> 30 minutes • You can watch them (all)/you can find out what is happening in the world <u>while/when/whilst/at the same time as</u> you are eating your <u>evening meal/dinner/tea</u> *NB: You can find out what is happening in the world in only 30 minutes = 1 mark*	2
	(b)		• News/it/they is/are <u>very well</u>-presented/commented/commentated/reported/covered <u>and</u> analysed OR • The news has <u>very good</u> commentary/commentaries/comments/coverage <u>and</u> analysis *Any one of above 2 points for 1 mark*	1
	(c)		• (Big) political debates/discussions in the run up to/approaching/near (the) election(s)/at election time • <u>Natural</u> disasters/catastrophes with brutal/frightening/scary/terrifying pictures/photos/images *NB: Big political debates in the run up to elections <u>rather than</u> natural disasters with brutal images = 1 mark*	2

Question			Expected response(s)	Max mark
4.			• They have/own/possess their <u>own</u> websites	1
5.			• (Older people) <u>continue to/still/keep</u> buy(ing) their <u>daily/everyday</u> newspaper (in kiosks or supermarkets)	1
6.			• They are interested in <u>local</u> events/events in the <u>area/neighbourhood/district</u>	1
7.			• They publish/print/release <u>photographs/pictures/images without permission/asking them</u> • They report/share details/publish/print/release/tell/talk about/write about <u>what</u> they eat for <u>breakfast</u> • (They report/share details/publish/print/release/tell/talk about/write) about <u>who</u> they went out with <u>last/previous week/the week before</u>	3
8.			Yes, it plays an important role because **+ a general reason** eg: • French people access a wide range of media (TV, Internet, newspapers) • The writer mentions positive and negative aspects of the media • All age groups access a form of media • The writer emphasises how long people spend using the media **+ a relevant example <u>which must back up</u> their reason** eg: • The young people access media online and older people read newspapers • They need the media to find out what is going on around the world • People watch news which can be educational but celebrities find the media intrusive • The writer suggests that celebrity magazines/reality TV are an escape from everyday life • The writer says that French people spend a minimum of three hours watching television *Assertion + reason = 1 mark* *Supporting **linking/relevant** examples = 1 mark*	2

Question 9 — Translation

The translation into English is allocated a maximum of **10 marks.** The text for translation will be divided into a number of sense units. Each sense unit is worth 2 marks, which will be awarded according to the quality and accuracy of the translation into English.

1	2 marks available:
Juliette Morelle qui prend le train tous les jours observe	Juliette Morelle who takes the train every day observes
Juliette Morelle qui prend le train	Juliette Morelle who takes/uses/gets the train
tous les jours	every day/on a daily basis
observe	observes/observed (stylistic expression)
	notes
	1 mark:
	Omission of who travels/goes by train
	and observes/watches
	0 marks:
	took
	Omission of every day
	all the days
	had observed/will observe/sees/to observe/any other tense

2	2 marks available:
«On voit les jeunes partout taper sur leur tablette	"One sees/you see young people everywhere (typing) on their tablet(s)
«On voit	"One sees/you see/we see
les jeunes	young people/youngsters
partout	everywhere
taper sur leur tablette	(typing/tapping/using) on their tablet(s)
	1 mark:
	Watch
	people/(the) youths/the youngsters/the young people/(the) teenagers
	always
	Omission of their
	0 marks:
	Omission of one/you/we see(s)
	saw (tense unless R.E.)
	to see
	watched
	children/infants
	Omission of everywhere
	banging/slamming/hitting
	put their tablets on
	all their tablets
	device(s)/phone(s)

3	2 marks available:
tout en regardant les émissions d'hier soir	while watching last night's programmes/shows
tout en regardant	while watching
les émissions	programmes/shows
d'hier soir	last night's/yesterday evening's/(the) programmes from the night before
	1 mark:
	all while
	Omission of while
	and watching the
	as they watch
	yesterday night
	0 marks:
	always/all
	to watch
	all (in) watching
	as they watched
	Omission of last night/evening
	emissions/channels

4	2 marks available:
qu'ils ont téléchargées.	(which/that) they (have) downloaded
	1 mark:
	which they had downloaded
	0 marks:
	are downloading/that are downloadable/they would download
	Position of last night eg they downloaded last night

5	2 marks available:
Je dois dire que le bruit incessant m'énerve énormément. »	I have to say (that) the incessant noise annoys me enormously/greatly."
Je dois dire que	I have to/must say (that)
le bruit incessant	the incessant/the unceasing/the constant/the non-stop/persistent/never-ending noise
m'énerve	annoys/irritates/bugs me/gets on my nerves
énormément. »	enormously/greatly/massively/hugely/tremendously/a great deal."
	1 mark:
	I need to say (that)/I must admit (that)
	a lot/really
	0 marks:
	inceasing/instantly
	Omission of incessant
	annoyed/enerves me
	edgy
	makes/puts me on edge
	environment

Directed Writing

Please refer to pages 93—94 for advice on the general marking principles for Higher French — Directed Writing.

Section 1 — Listening

Item 1

Question			Expected response(s)	Max mark
1.	(a)		• I am <u>no longer</u> a baby/I'm not a baby <u>anymore</u> • Holidays with the family are boring/they find them boring/it is boring • I miss my friends *Any two of above three points for 2 marks*	2
	(b)		• Take/make his/her/their <u>own</u> decisions • Make his/her/their <u>own</u> mistakes *NB It is acceptable to have 'own' once. For example 'make their own decisions and mistakes' = 2 marks*	2
	(c)	(i)	• <u>Language/linguistic</u> holidays/trips • Staying with <u>a</u> family/holiday with <u>a</u> family *Any one of above two points for 1 mark*	1
		(ii)	• Perfect/improve a language • Discover/experience/understand another/different/a new culture(s) *Any one of above two points for 1 mark*	1
	(d)		• <u>Feel</u> safe/secure/a <u>sense of</u> security • (Parents) <u>pay</u> for <u>everything</u>/<u>everything</u> is <u>paid</u> for OR • <u>Pay</u> for food/accommodation/activities (need 2 details)	2

Item 2

Question			Expected response(s)	Max mark
2.	(a)		• (She was very active and) she liked being outdoors/in the fresh air/outside • She was an only child/had no brothers or sisters <u>and</u> had nobody to play with OR • She was <u>less</u> alone/lonely/on her own	2
	(b)	(i)	• Painting • (Playing) board games	2
		(ii)	• (Learn to) play <u>together</u> • (Learn to) work as a <u>team/teamwork/groupwork</u> *Any one of above two points for 1 mark*	1

Question			Expected response(s)	Max mark
	(c)		• She <u>helped</u> the <u>younger/youngest/young</u> ones/children/people • When they had problems/if they had problems/with problems/when they were homesick/when they missed their parents	2
	(d)	(i)	• He did not talk/speak <u>much/a lot</u>/he <u>hardly/barely</u> talked/spoke • He did not <u>want</u> to take part/participate/join in (in the activities) *Any one of above two points for 1 mark*	1
		(ii)	• She spent (a lot of) time with him • She talked/chatted/spoke to him a <u>lot/lots/often/frequently</u> *Any one of above two points for 1 mark*	1
	(e)		• She has a meeting/a get together/meets/gets together with <u>colleagues/(fellow/other) workers/leaders</u> OR • She discusses/plans/talks about/figures out the timetable/programme of activities <u>for the next day</u> • Supervise/look after/keep an eye on/watch the children at meal times or any specific meal/when they eat	2
	(f)		• It is a region/area/place she does not know (at all)/is not familiar with • (She has learned Spanish and) is hoping/wishes/wants/would like to/will be able to/is able to/can go to Spain (during her holiday) *Any one of above two points for 1 mark*	1

Section 2 — Writing

Please refer to pages 95—97 for advice on general marking principles for Higher French — Writing.

HIGHER FRENCH 2018

Reading

Question			Expected response(s)	Max mark
1.			• Those who want to get away/ go/be (far) away/move away from/distance/detach/remove <u>themselves</u> from worry/worries/ concerns/stress of work • Those who want/like to go/be off the beaten track/path *Any one of above two points for 1 mark.*	1
2.			• <u>Relax/rest/chill out/unwind</u> on the (beautiful white sandy) <u>beach(es)</u> with a <u>coconut</u> (flavoured) <u>cocktail</u> • <u>Visit/go to numerous/many/a lot/lots/a number of natural/ nature</u> and <u>historical/history</u> attractions (for those who don't want to spend all their time on a beach) • <u>Taste/try/sample delicious/ tasty/savoury/spicy</u> (little) dishes/tapas + an example Fish in/with/and mango/mango (flavoured) fish (idea of a combined dish) **OR** Rice + spiced/flavoured with ginger/ginger rice	3
3.	(a)		• Their budget was <u>too</u> tight	1
	(b)	(i)	• (It was cheaper to do) research <u>on-line/on the internet</u> (before going)	1
		(ii)	• So that they would know exactly what they wanted to see <u>and</u> do (there) **OR** • It was cheaper <u>than going to a tour operator</u>	1
4.			• They had not reserved/booked a room in advance/before going/ earlier • They had to sleep on/at the beach • Mosquitoes/midges bit/annoyed/ irritated/bothered them <u>all night</u> *Any two of above three points for 2 marks.*	2
5.	(a)		• (Pretty, little) <u>remote/isolated/ hidden/tucked away</u> villages (in the tropical forest) **OR** • (Pretty, little) villages (nestled) <u>in the heart/in the depths of the</u> (tropical) <u>forest</u>	1

Question			Expected response(s)	Max mark
	(b)		• <u>Rare/endangered species/types/ kinds</u> of birds **OR** <u>Species/types/kinds</u> of <u>rare/endangered</u> birds • <u>Numerous/many/lots of/a large/ huge variety/varieties/kinds/ types</u> of orchids	2
	(c)	(i)	• You can do <u>walks/hikes/treks of different (skill) levels/standards</u> (of difficulty) **NB: idea of levels of difficulty not geographical levels within the forest** • To see/observe <u>wild</u> lemurs/ lemurs in the <u>wild/in freedom/ wandering freely</u>	2
		(ii)	• You (help) conserve/preserve the (natural) heritage (sites) (which is) endangered by deforestation **OR** You contribute to the conservation/preservation of the (natural) heritage (sites) (which is) endangered by deforestation	1
6.			• They took a/the wrong road/ route/turn(ing)/went the wrong way/they made a mistake on the road <u>during a tropical storm</u> • They <u>started/began</u> to panic • (After several kilometres) they noticed/glimpsed/saw/spotted/ caught sight of/came across/ upon a (small) house • A (hospitable) family took them in/put them up/gave them a room/accommodation/shelter <u>for the night</u> (to provide shelter from the rain) *Any three of above four points for 3 marks.*	3
7.			Yes, the writer recommends holidays in Madagascar (with a few hesitations) + **a general reason eg:** • The article is overwhelmingly positive. • The writer gives many advantages. • There are more positives than negatives. • The good points outweigh the bad. • The title is positive (referring to a paradise). • The idea of the island being like a paradise.	2

Question	Expected response(s)	Max mark
	+ a relevant example <u>which must back up</u> the assertion eg: • Beautiful scenery: white sandy beaches, pretty, little villages, it looks like a paradise. • Varied wildlife: the rare species of birds, the large variety of orchids. A walker and photographers' paradise. • Culture: variety of foods and drinks, welcoming people. *Assertion + reason = 1 mark* *Supporting linking/relevant examples = 1 mark*	

Question 9 – Translation

The translation into English is allocated a maximum of **10 marks**. The text for translation will be divided into a number of sense units. Each sense unit is worth 2 marks, which will be awarded according to the quality and accuracy of the translation into English. In assessing the candidate's performance, the descriptions detailed below will be used. Each sense unit will be awarded one of the marks shown.

1 *Située à neuf cents kilomètres de l'Afrique du Sud,*	*2 marks available:* Situated 900 kilometres from South Africa, Located away from South Africa *1 mark:* of/off South *Africa* situated at/found/around *0 marks:* any wrong number/distance eg miles (from) the south of Africa south of Africa
2 *Madagascar attire un grand nombre de touristes de tous les coins du monde.*	*2 marks available:* Madagascar attracts a large number of tourists from all corners of the world draws (in) entices lures a big/great number a large amount from all/the (fours) corners of the world/globe <u>all</u> areas/parts of the world/globe <u>every</u> part/area of the world/globe *1 mark:* brings in large numbers huge/substantial number from (all) across/around/over the world

	0 marks: welcomes a grand number lots of omission of a large number omission of world countries regions
3 *Il n'est pas difficile de voir pourquoi.*	*2 marks available:* It is not difficult/hard to see why. *0 marks:* the reason (on its own) Omission of why It's not to see why (omission of difficult)
4 *Selon les guides touristiques, on peut s'attendre à être ému*	*2 marks available:* According to (the) tourist guides you can expect to be moved tour guides you/we/one/people can expect to be... touched *0 marks:* following I/he/she/it/they you can wait you/we/one/people are able to Any other tense Omission of expect excited/graced Any reference to emus
5 *par l'accueil chaleureux qu'on recevra dès son arrivée.*	*2 marks available:* by the warm welcome you (will) receive as soon as you arrive. by the warm welcome (that/which) you (will) receive on arrival/when you arrive *1 mark:* by the warmth of the welcome by a warm welcome to be warmly welcomed warm reception from the warm welcome mixing of pronouns eg you will receive a warm welcome when one arrives to be met with (instead of receive) after/once you have arrived (verb error) from your arrival from the moment you arrived *0 marks:* lovely welcome any mention of reception desk omission of welcome by the warm welcome on arrival (omission of verb)

Directed Writing

Please refer to pages 93—94 for advice on the general marking principles for Higher French — Directed Writing.

Section 1 — Listening

Item 1

Question		Expected response(s)	Max mark
1.	(a)	• Between 30 minutes and one hour/30 minutes to one hour	1
	(b)	• The phone number of the <u>company/workplace/business/ enterprise</u> • The <u>name/contact details of the person(s) you are going to meet/the person(s) who is/are interviewing you</u> (in case you have a problem)	2
	(c)	• The <u>important points/things</u> in your CV • Why you are applying for the post/job/why you want the post/ job/why you have chosen to go for the post/job	2
	(d)	• (Personal questions on) your skills/abilities/competences (accept singular) • Your <u>previous/past/prior</u> experience/the experience you have/work experience/ experience of that type of work • Responsibilities in another job *Any two of the above three points for 2 marks*	2
	(e)	• Ask (a) question(s) about the <u>working/job conditions</u> (but it is not obligatory)	1

Item 2

Question		Expected answer (s)	Max mark
2.	(a)	• In the/a village bakery/the/a bakery in her village	1
	(b)	• There was a <u>car</u> accident/crash • The road/route was closed/ blocked/shut off • She was <u>15 mins</u> late (and she gave a bad impression of herself) *Any two of the above three points for 2 marks*	2
	(c)	• She was wearing sports clothes (the interviewers were wearing suits) • Her phone rang <u>twice</u> (because she forgot to switch it off)/The phone rang <u>twice</u> because she forgot to switch it off	2

Question		Expected response(s)	Max mark
	(d)	• She didn't <u>know how to/ couldn't</u> answer/respond to the question(s) • Her answers were (too) <u>short</u> (accept singular)	2
	(e)	• Her friend will <u>help</u> her to <u>prepare/get ready</u> (for the interview) **NB Ignore tense and ignore plurals**	1
	(f)	• She can sleep in the morning/ have a long lie **OR** People on holiday/tourists are relaxed • (She loves ice-cream so) she can eat as much ice-cream as she wants/whenever she likes	2
	(g)	• She will be able to travel/cycle around/move around/get around (in town) (more) easily/freely • She would be able to avoid <u>traffic jam(s)/congestion</u> • She would be able to keep in shape/keep fit *Any two of the above three points for 2 marks*	2

Section 2 — Writing

Please refer to pages 95—97 for advice on general marking principles for Higher French — Writing.